MOVERS,
SHAKERS,
& HISTORY
MAKERS

MICHAELA DePRINCE
FROM WAR-TORN CHILDHOOD TO BALLET FAME

CONTENT CONSULTANT
KATE MATTINGLY, PhD
ASSISTANT PROFESSOR
SCHOOL OF DANCE
UNIVERSITY OF UTAH

BY CARRIE MYERS

CAPSTONE PRESS
a capstone imprint

Capstone Captivate is published by Capstone Press, an imprint of Capstone.
1710 Roe Crest Drive
North Mankato, Minnesota 56003
www.capstonepub.com

Library of Congress Cataloging-in-Publication Data
Names: Myers, Carrie, author.
Title: Michaela DePrince : from war-torn childhood to ballet fame / Carrie Myers.
Description: North Mankato, Minnesota : Capstone Press, 2021. | Series: Movers, shakers, and history makers | Includes index. | Audience: Grades 4-6
Identifiers: LCCN 2020001167 (print) | LCCN 2020001168 (ebook) | ISBN 9781496684806 (hardcover) | ISBN 9781496688224 (paperback) | ISBN 9781496685001 (pdf)
Subjects: LCSH: DePrince, Michaela—Juvenile literature. | Ballet dancers—Sierra Leone—Biography—Juvenile literature. | Ballet dancers—United States—Biography—Juvenile literature. | Orphans—Sierra Leone—Biography—Juvenile literature.
Classification: LCC GV1785.D37 M84 2021 (print) | LCC GV1785.D37 (ebook) | DDC 792.802/8092 [B]--dc23
LC record available at https://lccn.loc.gov/2020001167
LC ebook record available at https://lccn.loc.gov/2020001168

Image Credits
AP Images: Denis Farrell, cover (foreground); Dance Magazine: May 1979 Dance Magazine cover. Reprinted with permission from Dance Magazine, 8; Getty Images: Ian Gavan/Getty Images Entertainment, 39, Jeff Vespa/WireImage, 31; Newscom: Jonas Gustavsson/NameFace/Sipa U/, 27, Jordi Matas/Polaris, 32, 35, Jose Luis Villegas/Zuma Press, 28, Malcolm Linton/KRT, 11, Sarah J. Glover/KRT, 22, Zero Creatives Cultura, 43; Red Line Editorial: 15; Rex Features: Gallo Images/Shutterstock, 5; Shutterstock Images: Christos Georghiou, 20, Flightseeing-Germany, 12, Iakov Filimonov, 19, Igor Bulgarin, 17, k_samurkas, 37, Leonardo Viti, 6, Monarexx, cover (background), 1

Editorial Credits
Editor: Marie Pearson; Designer: Colleen McLaren

Printed in the United States of America.
PA117

CONTENTS

Words in **bold** are in the glossary.

CHAPTER ONE

BORN INTO A WAR

When Michaela DePrince was born, no one would have guessed she would grow up to be a world-famous ballerina. And her name wasn't Michaela yet. Back then, it was Mabinty Bangura.

Michaela was born on January 6, 1995, in Sierra Leone, a country in West Africa. Her father said her birth was the highlight of his life. Michaela was born with a condition called **vitiligo**. It caused white spots on her dark brown skin. Other children were afraid of her. Her parents believed no one would marry her when she grew up because of her skin. Many people in Sierra Leone thought a curse caused vitiligo. Michaela's father believed that education was especially important for Michaela so she could support herself. He began to teach her the Arabic alphabet when she was just a toddler.

Michaela DePrince has danced all over the world. In 2012, she appeared in *Le Corsaire* in South Africa.

Freetown is Sierra Leone's capital city. Sierra Leone is home to more than 6.6 million people.

WAR ORPHAN

At the time, Sierra Leone was in the middle of a **civil war**. It lasted from 1991 until 2002. A group of people were fighting against the government. The group called itself the Revolutionary United Front. Its members were so violent that people gave them a new name. They mixed *devils* and **rebels** to get *debils*.

When Michaela was 3 years old, the debils came to her village. They killed all the workers in the diamond mines, including her father. Michaela and her mother went to live with her Uncle Abdullah. He treated them very badly. They never had enough to eat. Soon, Michaela's mother caught a fever and died. At the gravesite, Michaela cried. She wanted to be buried with her mother. Then Uncle Abdullah decided he would no longer care for Michaela.

ORPHAN NUMBER 27

Abdulla left Michaela at an orphanage in another town. She was still only 3 years old. One of the women who took care of the orphans was called Auntie Fatmata.

Michaela found a 1979 issue of *Dancemagazine*. It was how she learned about ballet.

Fatmata called the 27 orphans by numbers, not names. Her favorite was Number One. Michaela was her least favorite, so she made Michaela Number 27. Fatmata was cruel to Michaela and sometimes hit her.

There was another girl named Mabinty at the orphanage. She was the same age as Michaela. This other Mabinty was Fatmata's Number 26. On Michaela's first night, Mabinty comforted her and sang her to sleep. The two girls became best friends.

THE DANCING LADY

Around that time, Michaela found a magazine stuck in the orphanage gate. On the cover was a white woman wearing a short pink skirt and silky pink shoes. She had glitter on her clothes. She was standing on the tips of her toes. She had a big smile. Michaela decided she wanted to dance like the woman in the picture. She wanted to be happy like the dancer.

Michaela tore off the magazine cover. She folded it and hid it in her underwear. That was the only place she could keep it safe.

SIERRA LEONE ORPHANS

The civil war left many orphans. About 320,000 children lost their parents. Almost 50,000 lived in the streets. Since then, the country has had outbreaks of diseases. Even more children have lost their parents. Many organizations help Sierra Leone's orphans find sponsors. Sponsors help provide food, schooling, and medical care.

CHAPTER TWO

FLEEING THE DEBILS

A teacher named Sarah taught English and math to the children in the orphanage. She was sweet and smart and gave Michaela extra lessons. She reminded Michaela of her mother. Michaela showed Sarah her magazine picture. Sarah told Michaela that the dancing lady was called a ballerina.

One night, Sarah left the orphanage to go home. Some debils grabbed her. She was pregnant at the time. The debils killed her and her unborn baby girl. Michaela saw everything.

One of the debils also cut Michaela in the stomach. A guard from the orphanage begged the debils to let Michaela go. He saved her life. But Michaela felt so sad she almost didn't care.

The debils injured and killed many innocent people.

A few days later, the debils took over the orphanage. They made everyone leave. The director of the orphanage took the children to safety. He led everyone through a jungle and over mountains. Michaela brought her magazine cover with her. It gave her hope for a better life.

The children walked many miles to Guinea. This country borders Sierra Leone to the north and east. They stayed in a town called Conakry.

Conakry is the capital city of Guinea. The city lies on Guinea's coast.

A NEW FAMILY

One day, all the children flew to Ghana, another country in West Africa. There they would meet their new parents. Their new parents would take them to the United States.

All the other children in the orphanage had been chosen by families months ago. The children had family books filled with pictures and messages from their new parents. But no one had chosen 4-year-old Michaela. People did not want a child with vitiligo.

In the airport in Ghana, the children met their new families. Michaela stood with her arms folded. Then she saw a woman with shiny red shoes and white hair. The woman's name was Elaine DePrince. She was the mother from Mabinty's family book. She walked up to Michaela and Mabinty. She smiled and said that she was their new mother. Elaine had planned to adopt Mabinty. Then, before Elaine came to Ghana, she had learned that Michaela still needed a home, so she quickly agreed to adopt Michaela too. Michaela couldn't believe it. She and Mabinty would be sisters!

Elaine took the girls to a hotel room. Elaine's suitcases were like treasure chests. She had new clothes for the girls. She had brought dolls and beads. The girls each got sneakers with flashing lights on the heels. Michaela loved the sneakers. But one thing she wanted wasn't in the suitcases. She couldn't remember the English words for ballet shoes. So she showed Elaine her magazine picture. Elaine understood. She promised that when they arrived in the United States, Michaela would learn to dance.

Both girls were named Mabinty. Elaine thought that would be confusing. She renamed the girls Michaela and Mia. They both kept Mabinty as their middle names.

BELIEVING IN HERSELF

Many people told Michaela that she would never be adopted. Whenever people were mean to her, she told herself that it didn't matter what other people said. She would become someone important.

LOCATIONS IN MICHAELA'S EARLY LIFE

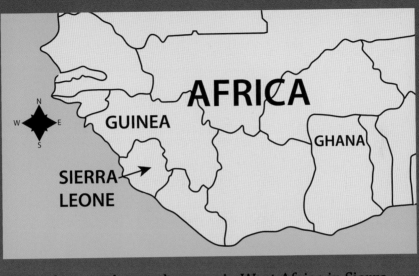

Michaela spent her early years in West Africa in Sierra Leone. Then she went to Guinea, and finally flew to Ghana, where she met her adoptive mother.

Michaela and Mia's new home was in Cherry Hill, New Jersey. Their new father was Charles DePrince. Elaine and Charles had adopted before. They also had two **biological** sons. Their oldest son was named Adam. He was grown and lived away from home. Erik and Teddy both still lived at home. Teddy was about 19. He became Michaela's favorite brother. By the time Michaela was grown, the DePrinces had adopted a total of nine children.

Ballet companies around the world perform variations of *The Nutcracker*.

During Michaela's and Mia's first summer in the United States, their dad gave each girl $2 to spend. Michaela spent $1 on a used ballet movie. It was George Balanchine's *The Nutcracker*. The New York City Ballet performed it. Some of Michaela's luggage hadn't made it to the United States. She lost her treasured magazine cover. *The Nutcracker* became its replacement. She watched it every day.

FUN FACTS ABOUT *THE NUTCRACKER*

- The ballet was based on the 1816 story *The Nutcracker and the Mouse King* by German writer E.T.A. Hoffman.

- Russian composer Pyotr Ilyich Tchaikovsky wrote the music for *The Nutcracker*.

- The first performance of *The Nutcracker* was in Russia on December 17, 1892. The critics did not care for it.

- In 1919, George Balanchine danced the role of the Prince in *The Nutcracker* in Russia. He was 15 years old.

- San Francisco Ballet held the first full-length performance of *The Nutcracker* in the United States in 1944.

- Balanchine arranged the dance for his own version of the ballet. It opened on February 2, 1954, in New York City. It was an immediate success.

- Today, many versions of *The Nutcracker* are performed around the world every year.

CHAPTER THREE

BALLERINA BEGINNINGS

On September 13, 1999, Michaela took her first dance lesson. It was a few months before she turned 5. Michaela wanted to do jumps and twirls. She wanted to balance on one foot and stick her other leg high into the air. But the class was full of girls who couldn't get basic positions right. Michaela was happy when it was time to try a new school.

A few days before Michaela's fifth birthday, Elaine signed Michaela up for lessons at the Rock School for Dance Education. Michaela met the director and stuck her leg straight up in the air. He was impressed. He placed her in a class for advanced beginners.

Young ballet students start learning basic skills. They learn more advanced skills as they become stronger.

GRAND JETÉ

ARABESQUE

PIROUETTE

PIXIE DUST

Michaela's skin embarrassed her. When she first bought a **leotard**, she chose a turtleneck with long sleeves. It covered the spots on her arms and shoulders. But it also made her hot and itchy. Her mother said that if Michaela became a professional ballerina, she wouldn't be able to wear long sleeves. After that, Michaela switched to a short-sleeved leotard.

Michaela still worried about her skin showing. At the end of her first semester at the Rock School, the school had a show. Michaela was in it. At intermission, Michaela asked her mother if she saw her spots. Her mother said she couldn't. From the audience, "they looked like a sprinkling of pixie dust." From then on, Michaela knew her spots wouldn't stop her from being a professional ballerina.

STRUGGLES IN AMERICA

When Michaela was 6, she got a new sister. Isatu had lived in the same orphanage as Michaela and Mia. Isatu's first adoptive home did not work out. So Michaela's parents adopted her. Michaela and Mia were both thrilled to have a new sister. Isatu wanted an *M* name to match her sisters. She chose the name Mariel.

Michaela's family (front row, left to right): Charles, Mariel, Elaine, Michaela, Mia. Standing behind them are Teddy and his girlfriend (left) and Adam and his wife (right).

Michaela, Mia, and Mariel had bad memories from the war. In their new life in the United States, men who wore camouflage scared them. So did men who spoke loudly or shouted. These men reminded them of debils.

Michaela also faced challenges in ballet. Her challenges weren't with the dancing. By the age of 7, she was ready to dance **en pointe**, or on her tiptoes. This is a huge step for ballerinas. It means they have strength. They also have technique, the ability to dance with precise movements.

FACT

Professional ballet dancers can wear out a pair of pointe shoes in one performance or less. An average professional dancer goes through 100 to 120 pairs every year.

From a young age, the challenges Michaela dealt with involved **racism** in her ballet classes. Most people in ballet were white. Michaela heard lots of negative comments about black dancers. Some comments came from parents and fellow students. These people said that black people didn't have the right type of body for ballet. She heard one of her directors say that black girls get too heavy as adults to be good ballerinas. These comments hurt Michaela.

TIGHTS AND POINTE SHOES

One way the world of ballet has quietly told black dancers that they are not welcome is with the color of ballet tights and pointe shoes. The preferred shade for ballet tights and shoes has always been pink. This color matches white skin. It can cause darker skin not to look smooth at a distance. Black dancers wanted more options that matched their skin. Today, more companies are making brown tights and pointe shoes, though they are still harder to find than pink ones.

When Michaela was about 8 years old, a professional dancer named Heidi Cruz-Austin helped her. She told Michaela she was a talented dancer and that Michaela should keep at it.

Michaela took Cruz-Austin's advice. At 8 years old, she tried out for the role of Marie in *The Nutcracker* at the Pennsylvania Ballet in Philadelphia. She didn't get the part. She overheard someone saying the city "wasn't ready for a black ballerina." Michaela was heartbroken. But she took another role and danced anyway. She wouldn't let racism defeat her.

HARDSHIPS

The hardest day for Michaela in America was yet to come. Her favorite big brother was Teddy. He teased and spoiled the sisters.

Teddy got sick and went to the hospital on November 13, 2004. It was the same day that the DePrinces officially adopted Amie. She was another girl from Sierra Leone. Teddy died later that night. He was only 24. Michaela gained and lost a family member at the same time. Michaela had never felt so sad. She hadn't realized that she could lose people in America too.

CHAPTER FOUR

SCHOOLING AND COMPETITIONS

Michaela quickly found success as a dancer beyond the Rock School. At age 10, she began training for the Youth America Grand Prix (YAGP). The YAGP is a ballet competition for dancers ages 9 to 19. Michaela won the Hope Award at the Philadelphia, Pennsylvania, semifinals in 2006. It was the top prize for dancers ages 9 to 11.

When Michaela was 12, she began winning summer **scholarships**. She spent the summer of 2007 with the Dance Theatre of Harlem in New York. For the first time, Michaela danced with a group of mostly black dancers.

Youth America Grand Prix competitions are held around the world. The finals are in New York.

The Dance Theatre of Harlem was founded in 1969. Its goal was to make ballet inclusive for all people.

Later that year, Michaela went on her first tour with a professional ballet company. A ballet company is a group of people who put on ballet performances. Michaela performed with the Albany Berkshire Ballet. She was one of the Flowers in the "Waltz of the Flowers" in *The Nutcracker*.

Shortly after the tour, Michaela turned 13. She won a scholarship to the American Ballet Theatre summer intensive. Elaine and Mia traveled with Michaela to New York City. They stayed in an apartment together. Michaela spent the summer of 2008 at American Ballet Theatre. At the end of the intensive, Michaela stayed for two more weeks to teach the 8-year-olds. She discovered she loved teaching children.

In January 2009, Michaela won the Youth Grand Prix, the top prize in her age group at the YAGP semifinals in Philadelphia. That summer, Michaela returned to the American Ballet Theatre. This time, her scholarship included both her school tuition and the cost of living in the city for the summer. She stayed in a dormitory—a building with shared bedrooms and bathrooms for students—with others in the program.

RISING FAME

When Michaela was 15, she competed in the YAGP finals in New York. A filmmaker named Bess Kargman wanted to make a film about seven dancers going to the 2010 finals. The finals attract more than 1,200 dancers from all over the world each year. Kargman wanted Michaela to be part of her film. At first, Michaela didn't want to. But her mom told her that participating could help make people aware that black girls can be good ballet dancers too.

At the YAGP, Michaela had **tendinitis** in her ankle. She was in terrible pain. She thought about quitting. But she didn't. She went on stage and danced her best. She earned applause from the audience and smiles from many of the judges.

FACT

Ballet dancing is so hard on the body that most dancers retire around age 40. But some people dance longer. Cuban ballerina Alicia Alonso danced professionally until she was 75.

Michaela (right) poses for a photo with Bess Kargman (center). Miko Fogarty (left) was also in Kargman's film.

The best dancers in the competition won invitations to join dance companies or scholarships to attend ballet schools. Michaela was one of them. She won a full scholarship to the American Ballet Theatre school in New York City. She could study ballet for free year-round. She continued her regular high school classes online.

Michaela was only 17 when she danced in *Le Corsaire*.

Kargman's film, *First Position*, came out in 2011. It was a big success. Michaela was interviewed by reporters from magazines, newspapers, and television shows.

In 2012, she was a guest on the TV show *Dancing with the Stars*. That same year, Michaela graduated from high school with honors. That summer, the South African Mzansi Ballet invited her to come to Johannesburg, South Africa. She danced her first professional role in the ballet *Le Corsaire*. The ballet is about pirates. Michaela danced as an enslaved girl named Gulnare. She was ready to become a full-time professional ballerina.

NO PAIN, NO GAIN

Like other athletes, ballet dancers' bodies can hurt from all the practice. Knee injuries are the most common. Ankle injuries and tendinitis are common too. And dancers' feet often blister and bleed while they are wearing pointe shoes.

CHAPTER FIVE

THE DUTCH NATIONAL BALLET

At age 17, Michaela began auditioning for classical ballet companies. At first, she didn't get any offers. The Dance Theatre of Harlem offered her a position for the 2012–2013 dance season. She accepted. A few days later, American Ballet Theatre offered Michaela a position. But it was too late. She was already committed to the Dance Theatre of Harlem. Michaela enjoyed her year. But the company was small. Her true dream was to dance with a major ballet company.

In December 2012, Michaela auditioned for the Dutch National Ballet in the Netherlands. Michaela worried that the director, Ted Brandsen, wouldn't accept a black dancer.

Michaela worked hard to accomplish her ballet goals.

But she found that skin color was less of an issue with European ballet companies. The Dutch National Ballet's dancers come from all over the world. Brandsen invited Michaela to join the junior company for 2013. She danced well enough to be placed as a second-year member even though it was only her first year. She would be an **apprentice** to the main company.

MOVING UP

In 2014, Michaela was promoted to the main company. Dancers in ballet companies have ranks, or positions. As they get more experience, they move up in rank. In the Dutch National Ballet, they start at élève, which is French for "student." That is where Michaela started. Dancers at this rank dance in large group scenes.

FACT

In 1990, Lauren Anderson at the Houston Ballet in Texas became one of the first black female dancers to hold the top rank of a major ballet company.

The Dutch National Ballet is based out of Amsterdam in the Netherlands.

A few weeks after her promotion, Michaela danced her first solo for the company. It was in *Swan Lake.* Brand new dancers in the company almost never get to perform solos. Michaela got the chance only because the original soloist, then another four dancers after that, all got sick or were injured. But everyone who watched her perform could see she belonged there.

When Michaela was growing up, people told her that her body was too athletic for her to dance graceful, delicate roles. But she saw white dancers with the same body type get those roles. She felt the problem was racism. She was thrilled to finally get the chance to prove everyone wrong.

CHAPTER SIX

SHARING HOPE

Michaela and her mother wrote a book about Michaela's life. Published in 2014, it was called *Taking Flight: From War Orphan to Star Ballerina*. Michaela felt she had been blessed with hope. She wanted to share that hope with others.

MEETING HER INSPIRATION

As Michaela gained more fame, she never forgot the ballerina who inspired her so many years ago. In 2014, a reporter helped her find the name of the ballerina. It was Magali Messac.

FACT

In addition to the United States, Michaela's book has been published in Brazil, France, Germany, Italy, Japan, the Netherlands, Poland, Portugal, Spain, and the United Kingdom.

Michaela hopes her story will inspire others.

Messac had danced with the Pennsylvania Ballet and appeared on a 1979 cover of *Dancemagazine.* When Messac heard Michaela's story, she wanted to give Michaela her copy of the magazine. The two met in July 2015 on a TV show. Michaela didn't know Messac would be there. The two women hugged each other hard. Michaela felt as if she had met her fairy godmother.

CONTINUED SUCCESS

Michaela advanced quickly at the Dutch National Ballet. In 2015, she became a coryphée. That meant that instead of dancing among a large group of dancers, she now danced with just a few others. That same year, a film company began planning a movie of Michaela's life.

AMAZING PERSON

Michaela has received recognition in the media for her work. In 2012, she was one of the Huffington Post's Most Amazing Young People of the Year. In 2017, she was named a *Today* show's *Today* Style Hero for her courage.

TRAILBLAZING BLACK BALLERINAS

1955: Raven Wilkinson becomes one of the first black ballet dancers to perform with a major ballet company.

1982: Debra Austin becomes the first black female principal dancer for a major ballet company, the Pennsylvania Ballet. Principal is the top rank in a ballet company.

1990: Lauren Anderson becomes the first black principal ballet dancer for the Houston Ballet.

2003: Aesha Ash rises to the rank of soloist, one of the top ranks, and today works to encourage other black ballerinas.

2015: Misty Copeland becomes the first black female principal ballerina with American Ballet Theatre.

In 2016, Michaela got to work with Beyoncé. The famous singer asked Michaela to create and perform her own dance for "Freedom," a music video from the album *Lemonade*.

Also in 2016, Michaela was promoted to grand sujet. This meant she would sometimes dance in groups, and other times dance solos by herself. Later that year, she became a soloist. She was only 20 years old.

SHARING HOPE

Michaela looked for more ways to share hope. She started teaching ballet. She wanted to inspire young black ballerinas to pursue their dreams. She began work with War Child, an organization that helps children living in war zones. Michaela visits countries such as Lebanon in the Middle East and Uganda in Africa. She performs dance recitals for children. She listens to their dreams and stories. Michaela started her own YouTube channel in 2017. She shares videos of her performances, talks, and fashion shoots. She talks about challenges such as needing surgery for an injury in August 2018.

In 2019, Michaela began work on a film version of the ballet *Coppélia*. She danced the lead role. The movie was being made by the Dutch National Ballet.

Michaela has had a lot of hardship in her life. But her love of ballet gives her a purpose. She works to pass that hope along to others. She wants people to be proud of themselves and to love their flaws and imperfections. They can have hope, just as she does.

Michaela encourages young girls to pursue their dreams.

TIMELINE

1995: Mabinty Bangura is born in Sierra Leone on January 6.

1999: Elaine and Charles DePrince adopt Mabinty and name her Michaela. Michaela has her first ballet lesson on September 13.

2009: Michaela wins the Youth Grand Prix at the Youth America Grand Prix semifinals in Philadelphia.

2011: Bess Kargman's *First Position* documentary is released.

2012: Michaela graduates from high school and joins the Dance Theatre of Harlem.

2012: Michaela completes her first performance as a professional ballerina with the South African Mzansi Ballet.

2014: Michaela and Elaine's book *Taking Flight: From War Orphan to Star Ballerina* is published.

2016: Michaela is promoted to grand sujet, and then to soloist with the Dutch National Ballet.

2019: Michaela dances the lead role in the film version of the ballet *Coppélia*.

**apprentice
(uh-PREN-tis)**
someone who learns a skill from a person who has mastered it

**biological
(by-uh-LAH-jih-kuhl)**
related through birth

civil war (CI-vul WOR)
a war between multiple groups in the same country

en pointe (ON PWANT)
dancing on the tips of one's toes

leotard (LEE-uh-tard)
a stretchy, tight-fitting, one-piece clothing item worn by dancers

racism (RAY-siz-uhm)
the belief that someone of a different skin color is inferior

rebels (RE-buls)
people who fight against a country's government or ruler

**scholarships
(SKAH-lur-ships)**
money awarded to students to help them attend school

**tendinitis
(ten-duh-NY-tus)**
inflammation of the tendon, the stretchy cord that connects muscle to bone

**vitiligo
(vih-tuh-LYE-go)**
a skin condition in which a person's skin has light spots

READ MORE

Copeland, Misty, and Brandy Colbert. *Life in Motion: An Unlikely Ballerina*. Young Reader's ed. New York: Aladdin, 2016.

Rissman, Rebecca. *Today's Ballet*. North Mankato, MN: Capstone Press, 2019.

Siegel, Siena Cherson. *To Dance: A Memoir*. Special ed. New York: Atheneum Books, 2019.

INTERNET SITES

American Ballet Theatre: Our History
https://www.abt.org/the-company/about/#history

Dance Theatre of Harlem: Our History
https://www.dancetheatreofharlem.org/our-history

Michaela DePrince: About
https://www.michaeladeprince.com/about-1

Quote Sources

p. 21, Michaela DePrince and Elaine DePrince. *Taking Flight: From War Orphan to Star Ballerina*. New York: Knopf Books, 2014 (ebook), pp. 95–96.
p. 24, Ibid., p. 133.